Think
Fearlessly

JUST ISAAC

BALBOA.PRESS
A DIVISION OF HAY HOUSE

Balboa Press books may be ordered through booksellers or by contacting:

Balboa Press
A Division of Hay House
1663 Liberty Drive
Bloomington, IN 47403
www.balboapress.com
844-682-1282

Because of the dynamic nature of the Internet, any web addresses or links contained in this book may have changed since publication and may no longer be valid. The views expressed in this work are solely those of the author and do not necessarily reflect the views of the publisher, and the publisher hereby disclaims any responsibility for them.

The author of this book does not dispense medical advice or prescribe the use of any technique as a form of treatment for physical, emotional, or medical problems without the advice of a physician, either directly or indirectly. The intent of the author is only to offer information of a general nature to help you in your quest for emotional and spiritual well-being. In the event you use any of the information in this book for yourself, which is your constitutional right, the author and the publisher assume no responsibility for your actions.

Any people depicted in stock imagery provided by Getty Images are models, and such images are being used for illustrative purposes only. Certain stock imagery © Getty Images.

Print information available on the last page.

ISBN: 978-1-9822-6413-0 (sc)
ISBN: 978-1-9822-6415-4 (hc)
ISBN: 978-1-9822-6414-7 (e)

Library of Congress Control Number: 2021903354

Balboa Press rev. date: 02/26/2021

CONTENTS

CONTENTS

ACKNOWLEDGMENT

I WOULD LIKE TO EXPRESS my special thanks of gratitude to Yeshua Messiah, for life and the completion of this project. The cultivation and guidance of one of the world's leading empowerment specialist visionary Dr. Bible Davids, you are one of the chosen. My dear friend and advisor the world-renowned Sophia Stewart, you are timeless. Dr. Cindy Trimm, thank you for the declarations over my projects. Another key motivator throughout this project, you're stuck with me through it all, my mentor, friend and one of the greatest trainers in the world Floyd Mayweather Sr., thank you for showing me how to fight. Uncle Ricky, Tina, Lorenzo, Zuleikha my prayer partner and greatest supporter, all of Motivational Fire, James Brown, Lorretta, Justin, Jeff Mayweather, Nicole, Brianna, Jimena, Karli, Grandma Gussie, Jadira, Angel, my precious son Elijah, Tye, Baby Alisha, I'm so proud of you, my good friend King James, The Pallard Family, The whole SL Protocol Team and family, Tim Storey, Chiara, Hector, Alisha, Roy Jones Jr, Austin, Gbenga, My Parents, I love you. All of my friends, family, and supporters. If I have not mentioned your name, and you have supported this project please forgive me. You are appreciated. XXX

CHAPTER 1

Free from Opinion

THERE ARE MOMENTS IN LIFE when we listen but do not hear, or when we hear but are not listening. Unless you are isolated from civilization, you will be constantly bombarded by information. There is nowhere on Planet Earth we can go where people do not transfer information. I remember sitting with a family member and friends in the living room of my grandmother's house. We were discussing our lifestyle values and goals. I was expressing my views on time management and how important every second of the day is to me. How it matters how I spend my time in life. My cousin turned to me in front of the whole family and stated that he had heard a rumor about my lifestyle. Many thoughts raced through my mind because of his statement. I then smiled, turned to him, and asked what the rumor was. He tilted his head to the side and looked at some of my other family members before saying, "I heard that you do not watch television."

I continued smiling as I looked at him and my other family members. The only sound I could hear were commercials playing from the television in the room. My cousin turned to me with a look on his face, much like he had medicine in his mouth. In other words, he looked as if he had just tasted something nasty. He went on to say, "It's really weird that you do not watch television. There is something really wrong with that."

I continued to smile as I squinted my eyes a little and thought about how to respond. The first thing that left my mouth was a burst of laughter. I could not hold it in any longer. By the time I was done with my belly laugh, my cousin was looking at me with a straight face, as if he was concerned about my well-being. The remote control was in his hand while the television was still running. There was a talk show on with people fighting and screaming loudly. I could tell that my cousin was having somewhat of a difficult time focusing on our conversation and watching the television at the same time. One eye was on the television and the other on me. It looked like he was watching a tennis match in the living room. I began to explain how when you watch television there are messages going out with no restraint. With television there is no engaging in dialogue. Instead, an internal dialogue is provoked after the viewer receives messages visually and audibly. The danger in having one-way communication is that only one opinion, view, and or mindset is expressed within the communication.

Many of us have embraced the culture of sitting in front of a box and absorbing everything that is projected. When I was a teenager, I had no understanding of the importance of what I watched. I did not understand that I would internalize the messages I received, and what I internalized would manifest in my life. Now that I have matured, I recognize that one value that keeps me balanced is aiming to do everything in moderation. There are times that I fall short, but I believe the first step in thinking progressively in this area is awareness. I believe that we should be open to others' opinions provided their opinions are conducive to our personal values. We are not cookie-cutt people; we each have individuality and a unique purpose.

Seeking the opinions of others on a frequent basis can be dangerous. What if I had listened to my cousin's opinion of me and had planned to watch television a minimum of seven hours a day? There are systems set up that drive the progress of many through television. I find it amazing how watching a movie can affect our vibrations (feelings) and thought patterns so much that it inspires something— good or bad—to manifest in our lives. I am not saying that I think television itself is evil or bad. But its lack of balance and awareness can corrupt all that we are and all that we will become through one-way communication or even a negative conversation, depending on the source. Before attempting anything good or great, we need to be mindful that people will have their opinions, and their opinions can affect us in good ways or in bad ways if we allow it. This is why it is vitally important to evaluate constantly those who are in our spheres of influence. The people we allow close to our hearts and minds can be tremendously impactful, to the point of altering our visions, purposes, dreams, goals, and destinies. Suggestive thoughts are seeds that can grow into something so significant that they define who we are. Opinions come in the form of words, and these words can keep us caged by fear or free us.

As you read this book, your subconscious awareness is being heightened to the point of understanding that you will no longer be held hostage by another person's opinion of you. There are standards that are being raised up that will ultimately smack fear out of your mindset and lifestyle. Have you ever thought of doing something daring? I'm not talking about putting your life in danger. What I am talking about is making a plan to fulfill a vision that scares the living daylights out of you because of all the obstacles and impossibilities surrounding it. There are whispering voices in your head that tell you what you can and cannot do. These voices stem from your childhood, your past, and current environment. They have their opinions about you, and it is up to you to decide whether you will allow someone else's negative ideas about you and what you desire to live or die. These voices are sometimes unconscious. We often cannot detect them unless we tune in to our emotional states. Whenever we feel negative—meaning down, discouraged, or hopeless—this may indicate that fear is standing in our pathways, attempting to block the fulfillment of our destinies and our joy along our journeys.

Bruce was one of my favorite fighters in my early childhood. I started taking martial arts at the age of six. There are many things that I remember about Mr. Bruce. He seemed to have a keen sense of focus while in training and during combat. I remember watching a scene with him walking down the road and being confronted by some opponents. I thought they looked very threatening. They served a purpose in meeting him on his path toward his desired destination. His opponents—or should I say, opposition—would reveal his DNA and ultimately the blueprint of his destiny in the story. If he had not been willing to fight through the opposition, he would have been beaten to death by adversity. I believe the other purpose the opposition or adversity served was to reveal the greatness that existed inside him.

Fear can come in the form of words that create an image in the mind of something happening. Fear is usually linked to trepidation, failure, or any other thoughts that invoke negative feelings. When Bruce was confronted with fear, he would start to dance on his toes and move around with a rhythm of his own. The way he did things was part of his branding and his legacy. He was intentional in attacking the hell out of his adversaries, and he did so with tenacity, consistency, focus, and accuracy until ultimately conquering what might have appeared unconquerable. He was hurt at times and even put down. But I loved how he pushed through and the loud smacking sound that was made before his opponents fell at his feet.

What is your desired destination? Are you willing to push through to see its manifestation? People may laugh at your ideas; they may use words of discouragement. There may even be gossip about the desire you have expressed. See yourself accomplishing what you set out to do. Speak aloud; tell yourself what you desire to accomplish. The words that we speak have future implications, and there is a process of conception that takes place in the mind. The words we speak over ourselves have the potential to override the voices of discouragement within our unconscious minds, or even the negative words other people use intentionally or unintentionally.

Get used to speaking what you desire to accomplish aloud and alone in a quiet place. Repeat these declarations with faith and feeling: "I believe in myself. I am successful. I am intelligent. I am working toward greatness. I love myself, and I am loved. I am focused. I have power to gain wealth and help other people. I am a beautiful person." Even if you do not believe what leaves your mouth right away, try repeating these declarations aloud twenty times, and watch what happens to your emotional state. If it is done with faith, you will notice that you feel encouraged.

It is good to remember that everyone works at a different pace. There is some deprogramming involved in this process, which is known as intentional suggestion. We are prone to suggestion when we repeat both negative and positive things about ourselves. Never speak negative words over yourself, even in a joking way. Do not tolerate anyone you interact with to speak negative words over you. You are special, and you are chosen for greatness. Close your eyes, and visualize to the point of feeling what it is that you have hoped for. Free yourself from the opinions of others.

Once you begin to think fearlessly, some of those around you will pick up your frequency of confidence. Some may resent your flow toward success. In all humility, you and I have the power of choice in every circumstance. This power is sometimes ignored or forgotten. You are free to be the best that you can be, you are free to pursue true happiness, you are free to live by your own values. And you are free to shut down every opinion that either yells or whispers words that do not correlate with your destiny. Grasp the awareness that the most significant factor to consider is not the opinions of others and how they see you. However, take into consideration the most important opinion is how you see and think of yourself.

CHAPTER 2

Uncover and Discover

I REMEMBER A TIME WHEN I did not want to crack my eyelids open in the morning. If I could have slept my life away, that would have been my choice. I believe that this emotional state was prompted by my thought life. I was often told as a child that I would never be anything in life. These words are better known as "word curses." I began to understand at an early age that I could use people's negative words spoken over me as fuel to propel me to a place of success. This was not an easy process in the beginning. At one point I began to believe that I was destined for failure. But as time went on, and through the experiences and circumstances that were out of my control, there were times the mysteries of success were revealed to me.

I have had many dreams, yet I have not had the privilege of failing in the pursuit of all of them. Failing can be evidence of someone trying something. But since I did not have the courage, the motivation, or a strong interest in going after what I dreamed of at times, I didn't fail openly. Or maybe subconsciously it was the fear of failure itself. Well, this is a new day, and I am ready once again to think fearlessly.

There are times when we may need a little help along the way when it comes to seeing things from a different perspective. This is not a contradiction of chapter 1, but it is a matter of remaining balanced. I believe if we have a habit of always looking to others for the answers to our questions, then this is not a balanced lifestyle. There are times when I pray or meditate until the answer comes intrinsically. I would best describe it as an internal impression. I would also say that circumstances point me in the right direction; I would describe this as divine intervention.

I remember when I was independently promoting a music project. I felt led to drive from Canada to Atlanta in a red Impala. I felt led to drive alone, and it was about a ten-hour drive. I packed my bags, not knowing how everything was going to play out. I connected with one of my favorite cousins, Lenora, who has lived in Atlanta most of her life with her husband and beautiful children. I had word that Rev Jakes was speaking, and there was a mega event. Other speakers from across the nation were supposed to be present as well. I also planned on selling my music project out of the trunk of my car. I did a music video for one of the songs in this particular project that had five million views on the debut, placing the video between 50 and Kanye. Eventually it went on heavy rotation, airing on multiple television stations across North America and on some European networks.

So I set out. I wish that I could say I was doing the speed limit the entire time. I put the pedal to the metal and practiced singing my music hour after hour. It really made the duration of the trip seem shorter, and I was thankful that I was never pulled over. When I finally arrived in Atlanta, I could feel the atmosphere shift. The energy just felt totally different from where I had come from. I arrived at my cousin's house and was welcomed with open arms. The hospitality of the South really exists.

The first morning of my stay in Atlanta I woke up to the smell of something delicious. I made my way to the living room and peeked around the corner. There was a table full of delicious food, all laid out beautifully. I saw grits, turkey bacon, oatmeal, pancakes, eggs, orange juice, apple juice, biscuits and gravy, and so on. This was something that happened all the days of my stay, and I have never forgotten it. I took this way of living with me and locked it into my lifestyle. Hospitality is something special in my eyes because it is an expression of the heart that touches people in a caring way. I love to watch people eat and enjoy something that I made. I would never have discovered these things if I had not of taken a leap of faith.

On our journeys in life, we encounter, discover, and/or uncover pleasant surprises that we never even imagined—if we are open to seeing them. I have learned that our perspectives in situations determine the outcomes. Allow optimism to override every fear or preconceived notion. Speak over your own life that every negative experience of the past will not lead or dictate your future. To discover and uncover new and exciting things, we must embrace a sense of creativity and openness to the idea of deserving something wonderful. The imagination has been given to each of us, and we all have different ways of imagining things. Take five to ten minutes a day to visualize the things that you would love to accomplish, the things that you would love to see happening in life. When you begin the visualization exercise, at first your mind may wander to things that are of less importance. But allow negative thoughts linked to fear or failure to fade away and be replaced with your innermost desire. The things that you truly desire deserve your attention. Allow yourself to feel emotionally connected to what it will be like when you are in that moment. Punch your way through fear, and you will see light on the other side. Let go of your past mistakes; ask for forgiveness for the bad choices that you made. You must know that you deserve the best.

Going back to my pleasant surprise of breakfast, I ate until I was comfortably full and then made my first phone call. Prior to leaving for Atlanta, I spoke to Holyfield's wife about my vision, so I reconnected with her. My initial objective was to discuss the possibilities of signing a deal on the heavyweight champ's record label. At the time I was noticing great movement in the roster of artists. Some were attending the most prestigious awards shows across the nation. We talked for a good while and planned to meet up with the champ while I was in the city, providing everything lined up as planned.

I set out to open shop on a strip on one of the busiest streets. My eye caught the perfect place for me to park. I pulled in the parking space and popped my trunk with music playing from my project titled, "Remember Me." Right away people came up to me and began listening and asking questions about my story. I did well with sales as well. I was there for hours, yet it seemed like minutes, not only promoting my project, but speaking good things into people's lives. I never knew I was going to have this type of high. I met hundreds of people, and I felt so alive doing what I love to do. I discovered that no matter how humble the beginnings are, if I am married to my purpose, there is a peace and joy that passes all understanding.

A man stopped in front of my car and asked for a CD, and I handed him one. He held it in his hand and began to look in the sky with a blank stare. He then said, "You know what?" When I asked him what, there was a long pause as he looked back at me, squinting. "You know where you should go?" I asked him where he thought I should go. "You should go where there are a bunch of journalists and tell them your story about boxing and the music industry." I asked him where he suggested, and he replied, "You should go to the Hyatt."

I thanked him for the information, and he walked away after purchasing a CD. I stood there as the traffic of people passing began to slow down. It was then that I began to pray for a sign if I should go to the hotel as the man suggested. The strangest thing began to happen. There was a sun shower over me and my car. It seemed not to be raining across the street, only where I was standing. So I made my way underneath the shelter of a submarine shop. I stood in front of the door, waiting for it to stop raining while the sun was shining. It slowed down a little, so I headed to my car. I hopped in and headed for the Hyatt. I did not have an invitation, but I pulled up. Top-of-the-line cars were waiting to be valet parked, so I decided to park on the street around the corner.

As I walked up to the doors, a big man with a headset was denying people entry. I began to pray quietly, and I ended up walking right by this six feet something security guard. I was dressed in jeans and a T-shirt and feeling like I looked so out of place. I went to ask for a bottle of water, and the person working behind the counter said that it was seven dollars for one bottle. The muffins and donuts were five dollars each. So I declined because of the principle, not because I did not have the money. I looked around, and all I saw were tuxedos and beautiful dresses. It made me even more aware that I was wearing jeans and a T-shirt.

I found a table off to the side, where I was not really seen by many. As I sat there, I started to feel more out of place, like I should not be there. So I said another prayer and asked God if I should be there. Then a woman walked up to me with the biggest, brightest smile on her face. She asked me what I was doing in the building. I pulled out a collage of pictures and a copy of my *Remember Me* CD. And then she asked, "What do you want, and what are you trying to do?"

"I want to be interviewed by a journalist," I replied.

She took out her tape recorder and placed it on the table. "Well here I am!" She introduced herself as Karen K. I was kind of taken aback at how assertive that she was. She began interviewing me right then and there. She had a spark in her eye as she talked to me with the biggest brightest smile. As she looked at my newspaper articles and read about my music project, she began to build into me. She reinforced the idea that I am an object of divine attention. A tear left my eye, and then tears began to roll down my cheeks like Niagara Falls. She then said, "You know what, you are coming with me!" Karen reached for my hand and pulled me in a direction where I was about to discover a pleasant surprise.

As we walked, I was cut off by another giant working security. With a voice that was so assertive that it could not be ignored, he said, "You wanna back up, sir!" He repeated this twice as he stuck his big hand out in front of me. His hand could cover most of my face. I stumbled back and looked to the side, just past him, in astonishment. I could not believe my eyes. Someone was sitting in a chair speaking with celebrities.

Oh, my goodness. I could not believe it. It was one of the most well-known activists and world-renowned leaders. I pointed because I recognized him. As I leaned to the side, he locked eyes with me and said, "Let the young man through," repeatedly. I looked behind me and on both sides, wondering who he was talking about. *No, not me,* I thought. *I mean, who am I?* He pointed at me, repeating, "Let the young man through. Come here, young man." I smiled, not knowing what was going to happen next. The security guard moved aside as I walked past him. I looked him up and down, smiling. I discovered when someone believes and receives by faith, nothing is impossible.

I walked toward Rev. Jackson as cameras from CNN, Fox, and other major networks were taking pictures of me walking toward him. He reached out his hand to shake my hand. All I could see was the flashing of the cameras and so many familiar faces. What happened next was not only incredible but somewhat humorous.

CHAPTER 3

The Truth in Giving, or How to Give

WE SHOOK HANDS AS MOST of the people in the place were focused on Rev. Jackson and our interaction. He had such a firm grip as he looked me directly in my eyes. I admit that I was somewhat starstruck because I had watched this man from my childhood on national television fighting for the rights of black people. And he also ran for president. As I shook his hand, all I could say was his name again and again. I eventually coughed out some information about my music project.

I also met some of the most influential people in the world. Another man, comedian and black activist Mr. Gregory, walked up to me and talked to me as if he had known me my whole life. He took my project and began asking me questions such as, "What was your purpose for doing this project?" The first purpose that I gave him for the project was that I wanted to reveal the truth to the masses. To succeed in life, we must *think fearlessly*. I believe ultimately that there are only two primary realms that exist within time. There is the realm of fear and then there is the realm of love. I will continue to emphasize that it is my belief that a realm is an actual place. We can live in the realm of fear, or we can live in the actual realm of love. There is a distinction between fear and respect or reverence, and it takes wisdom to be able to distinguish between the two. For instance, if we misuse something carelessly (no wisdom), there can be great consequences involved. If our perspective is missing the component of respect, in some cases this can also lead to consequences that are not in our favor. For instance, electricity can be used to for our convenience and save lives. However, if it is misused, it can end lives. There was a time when the idea of using electricity for our convenience seemed far-fetched. The truth was revealed by a man named Benjamin. If this man had listened to the doubters and spectators, he would have never made one of the most revolutionary contributions to our world.

As I was finishing my conversation with Mr. Gregory, Rev, Jackson looked over at me and said, "Go say hello to Will."

I had no idea who he was talking about. Then he pointed to a man sitting at the head of an extravagant table. He was smiling at me as I made my way over to him. I greeted him with a smile and asked, "How are you, sir?

He replied, "I'm doing really good."

Because I had an awareness that the room was full of influential people, I asked him a question that made him laugh as he hung his head down. "What do you do, sir?" He never answered the question. Others heard me in my ignorance and started laughing as well.

I looked around the room at the few people who could hear our conversation as they laughed. I had no idea why my question was so funny. I asked him once again, "What is your name, sir?"

With a southern accent, he replied, "Willie."

I asked him very respectfully, "What do you do, Willie?" A man walked up to me, put his hand on my shoulder, and told me he was a country singer. Suddenly, I remembered hearing his name. The truth is he was a very well-known singer. I had no idea that this man was so well known until after I was laughed at and informed.

In my humble opinion, I believe that we should always treat people with the utmost respect, not because of who they are status wise or what they have materially or financially, but because of the integrities of their hearts. We are known by our characters, which cannot be separated from our legacies. I notice a common characteristic among the people I met who have made great impacts on my life. I recognize that no one owes me anything. However, I am forever grateful for the people of influence who have taken time to engage me in a conversation, even if it was just for a few minutes. Time is valuable, and here were people who took time to show me attention when they did not have to. I believe that you and I must do the same with wisdom.

In your pursuit of success, do not forget the people you are currently connected to who may need a helping hand in their pursuits of success. Your time spent affirming someone's value while lifting the individual up could help him or her achieve new levels of success. When we become self-centered in our pursuits to advance in life, the joy of the achievement is only temporal. There is the old saying, "Selfish people are never happy, only people who give."

I believe that what we send out into the universe will come back. Picture yourself achieving a goal or fulfilling a vision. It is not complete if we are missing the process of giving something back in return. How important is it as part of your legacy for you to be remembered for giving and helping someone? In my opinion, that is the ultimate level of greatness. One of the greatest connections that we can have with others is maximizing their potentials or contributing something toward the fulfillment of their destinies.

Have you ever been in a place where you felt stuck, and someone came along and helped you to overcome what was keeping you from reaching your next level? One of the greatest fighters of all time, Ali, was so successful in the fight game that millions of people all over the world knew who he was. He was fearless at a time when black people were persecuted on a consistent basis, around the time of the civil rights movement. He understood the power of words and often used his gift of gab to shock his opponents in and out of the ring. Ali believed in himself and usually delivered what he spoke over his life. He defied all odds, winning fights most believed were impossible. When he defeated Foreman, Ali looked directly into the camera without fear, pointed his finger, and with such passion said, "I told you I'm the real champion."

George was at his prime when he lost his fight to the greatest. However, I noticed something significant about him that I could not ignore. Years later he admitted that the greatest was the better man that night. George gave something back! George gave credit and paid honor to someone who succeeded even at the expense of his temporary setback. George is now a very wealthy man, not just financially. He is an ordained minister who preaches about the good tithe and continues to give.

Fear did not stop Ali or George from achieving the impossible. The average man would have folded out of fear after looking at the stature of the opposition that Ali faced in and out of the ring. Ali refused to fight a war that he did not believe in, and he was ridiculed by the masses for his decision. He was labeled many things and looked at in the worse way by many. But he had his reasons, and years later, he would be celebrated because of his decision. He did not allow the fear of rejection or even the imprisonment of his body to rule his life. Here was a man who was stripped of almost everything possible, but his belief system could not be taken from him. There were many who wanted to see him fail, and there were many who wanted to see him succeed. Regardless, Ali was not held hostage by society's opinion of him. He could have became self-centered and bitter toward society to the point of neglecting his own values. However, his belief system maintained the component of giving. He was not only fearless in giving his all during training with a competitive edge, he was also known for giving to others who were in need. One of his famous quotes, which I will never forget, is, "When you give something to others, that is the rent you pay for space living on earth."

He lived during an era when black people were publicly despised and rejected. They were physically attacked on the streets without cause. However, he used his words to speak out against the injustices that existed in the United States of America. Ali received threats that could have caused him to close his mouth without saying a word about how he felt and what he thought. But he was courageous in his pursuit of casting light on the very dark circumstances involving the conditions and mindsets of humanity living in the western world. He took action along with the words that he used, and those words came from a place of desire.

When we are thirsty, we drink. When we are hungry, we eat. There was a desire to see change in how certain things were done, and this was expressed with what I call verbal combat. My question for you is, "What are your desires?" What would you like to see happen through your life? And if you knew that what you spoke had great potential to manifest, would you begin speaking things that you desire without fear until you see what you hoped for begin to form? We must remember that what we allow to pass through the gates of our eyes and stream in our minds has a very high chance of dominating our thoughts and will often be expressed through the words that we speak. Therefore, I will continue to emphasize the importance of what we listen to and watch. They could ultimately make the difference in the fulfillment of our destinies. One of the biggest reasons is that the words that leave our mouths most likely correlate with what we are thinking. Are you ready for your words to be influenced by your thoughts and for your words to be an influence on others? Are you ready to think fearlessly?

CHAPTER 4

Every Step

THERE WILL DEFINITIVELY BE TIMES when our hearts and minds will be tested by fear. When we are challenged by something with the element of fear, it can reveal courage. There are also times the element of fear can be prevalent when we choose to say no to a challenge that may not be good for us. In my opinion, this can reveal courage as well. Not accepting a challenge that compromises our values is linked to integrity, and can also reveal someone's courage. It does not feel good to know when fear has gotten the best of us. However, moments like these can be self-teachable moments where we can learn from our mistakes.

Living in fear can be a very miserable place, especially when someone who is fearful tries to transfer the frequency of fear to the next person. I remember reading a biblical passage where a man named Peter was on a boat with his dudes during a storm. When there is a storm, we can feel a power that surrounds us, and it can be intimidating at times. Everyone on the boat was concerned about the crazy weather.

It is my belief that the storm represents circumstances in life that are out of our control. I can visualize the waves rocking the boat. There was a full moon, the wind was blowing, and the thunder was so loud that it shook the boat. And every few minutes there must have been the flashes of lightning reflecting on their wet faces. The pouring rain beat hard against the water, drowning out their voices as they tried to communicate with each other. When there is fear, there is also confusion, frustration, anxiety, and an innermost desire to avoid or overcome a negative possible outcome.

In the middle of the storm a man was seen walking on the water; he evidently conquered the elements of the world that surrounded him. Those on the boat began to scream and point in fear. In their hearts they trembled because they saw someone doing something that had never been done before. The focus of fear left from the storm and turned toward the one walking on the water during the storm. I visualize them pointing and saying that this cannot be real. It's a ghost, an illusion, no one could possibly defy these limitations. Many today would say this could only happen in the movies because we are told from childhood that it is impossible to walk on water, to be wealthy, to change lives, to do something daring, to leave a legacy with an impact that can be remembered for generations.

The miracle was more than just defying the laws of physics. There was a great connection made by this man who walked on water with someone watching from the boat. Peter saw the situation as an opportunity to be a follower of greatness, while the other men on the boat were preoccupied by fear. He recognized the opportunity though he knew odds were against him. The first step in accomplishing anything is to visualize what it is that we would like to accomplish.

There will be the noise of the naysayers, the doubters, the ones who are safe on their little boat, the ones who will never step out to try anything daring. Peter was like you and I, willing to step out despite the noise of those who surround us and tell us how hard it will be. They may talk to you about how many people have tried to accomplish the same thing and have failed.

Peter experienced an inner battle going on, one side telling him to join in with everyone else's view of his situation and the other to take a step of faith. Through all the silent chaos that was going on intrinsically (internally), he called out to the one walking on the water, "If it is you, the one I know, tell me to come." I can imagine the look on the faces of the people surrounding him. They probably thought, *This dude is trippin'. What the heck is he talking about? We are in a storm, and he is actually talking about taking a chance, knowing that there is the potential of failure or disappointment.*

We know what Peter visualized by his first statement. His Savior was involving him in a situation (the storm) that involved him doing something daring. "If it's you, the one I know, tell me to come," and the response to Peter was, "It is I, so come." Peter stepped out of the boat and on to the water. He began to walk, and his momentary dream of doing something daring turned into reality as he defied the laws of physics. He followed greatness, not just through emulation, but through his heart. Step after step he took in raw power until he began to look at the storm (distraction) like the rest of us do at times. I could picture him even looking back at how far he had walked away from what he knew as a familiar place, the boat. Some of his dudes were in shock that he went that far, and some told him he should come back.

When Peter began to lose focus of the one calling him out to do something daring, he began to sink. I can hear those on the boat screaming at Peter, "See, I told you so! Look at you now! You had a good job, you had security, why would you leave your comfort zone for your dream?" The second Peter began to look at what could happen in a bad way—most likely after listening to his dudes yelling, "Come back to us"—he lost focus of the Savior who conquered it all called him out to do the same. As Peter began to sink, he cried out in fear and reached out his hand for support. In a previous chapter I talked about the importance of reaching out to lend a hand when someone is in need. The second Peter reached out his hand, the Messiah was there with a strong arm to lift him out of his despair.

This is a representation of hope. Hope is when we see what we have access to. It may take some time to manifest, but do not be afraid to step out of a place of comfort to fulfill your destiny. The real war is found in speaking over the voices from within that tell us anything negative. Which report that we believe will affect the outcome of every situation. If you find yourself having a hard time getting started on a project or goal, setting a deadline can sometimes be a good thing. Putting a little pressure on yourself can help you to begin your steps toward the fulfillment of your vision and purpose. Setting a deadline can create motivation, providing it is a realistic one. The fact that you have picked up this book, which is stimulating your thoughts and activating your awareness of who you are, is a miracle.

You are a jewel, a diamond in the process. And let us not forget what it takes to produce a diamond. It takes thousands of years of heat and pressure. The things in which you have experienced throughout life—the pain, the heartache, the rejection, the betrayal, two-faced people, disappointments, failure—are all components with the potential to create something in us that prosperity can never produce. But only if we have the right attitudes and understandings. Happiness is only understood if we have experienced sadness. We are thirsty, so our thirst can be quenched, we are hungry until we eat, we are tired until we rest, we are sleepy and experience sleep. Likewise, joy would not feel so good if it weren't for pain. Our ignorance is revealed when our understanding of the knowledge given to us is opened before us.

There is nothing that is unattainable for you. There are opportunities waiting to be discovered. If you are sure of the direction that you would like to take but do not have a clue on how to navigate through the process of fulfilling a vision, be mindful that it takes creativity. Even if you are reading this book and have battled with fear in any sense, or if you have no clue about the direction that you would like to take in life, search for information online about what interests you. Reading about things that interest you or that you are involved in will likely spark the creativity already inside you. Every step we take toward fulfilling a vision or purpose is meaningful. Even the small steps that we take add up. Any successful person has had to take steps.

There are times when our visions, purposes, or goals evolve. There have been times in my own life when I have given up on a goal in my own mind, even before becoming active in pursuit of it, because I was in a place of fear involving future failure. I am learning to start taking steps when a thought is conceived that correlates with my values. There are things in the past that I set out to do, even to the point of becoming active in attempting to achieve a goal, but changed my mind because I recognized they did not correlate with my values or destiny. However, one of the worst things that we can do is to allow someone else to influence us through fear and terminate our vision or goal.

Because you and I have made poor choices or bad decisions in the past does not disqualify us from achieving goals and reaping the benefits of success. I encourage you to make verbal declarations to yourself in a secret place where no one else can hear: "I deserve to be happy. I will succeed in achieving my goals. I am intelligent, beautiful, insightful, and loved. My mind is sharp, my body is healthy and strong, and I attract people in my life who will help me to fulfill my vision, goals, and purpose. I choose to think fearlessly toward fulfilling my destiny of greatness."

CHAPTER 5

Influence

WHAT THE MIND IS CONTINUOUSLY filled with is what we allow to dominate our thoughts. It is then that we see manifestations of what we meditate on through faith. This is the process of thoughts becoming the things we have envisioned. You can smack fear so hard out of your thoughts that all you have left are ears to hear clearly good thoughts that will propel you to greatness. It is the awareness and ability to exercise the visualization of what it is we desire. We have over 60,000 thoughts in a day, and the origin of the majority of them are imposed by external forces. In my opinion, the greatest force that exists within the realm of earth is the power of influence. From my limited understanding, influence can be facilitated in the form of actions or words 99 percent of the time. There were men who almost took over the entire world through the power of influence. One man once said, "Words are bridges to regions unexplored." Is this statement good or evil in essence? The source of this statement is only defined by the person's functionality behind what is being said. The man who made this statement was Hitler.

Influence can be good or evil depending on its application. How words are used or received determines the level of influence projected and the outcome. Evidently Hitler used this principle in an evil way. It is my belief that words have the potential of having a tangible presence on them. The power of repeatedly encouraging oneself can be the most powerful influence in the world. It's not what people say about you that should matter most. It is what you say about yourself that really counts. People will have opinions about who you are or what you can accomplish based on many factors, including their own experiences, influences, backgrounds, cultures, DNA, and more. We need to be mindful of the people closest to us because they have access to our hearts and minds. Their influence can make or break us when it comes to success or failure. We constantly need to be mindful of the words of people who are around us.

When we have conceived a vision mentally, we can allow it to grow within us as it is nurtured and fed good things. However, if we are not careful, we can also partake in the termination of a viable vision because of negative influences. When I began to work as a recording artist, I knew that I would encounter some people who would try to discourage me from reaching for my dreams. I also felt optimistic because I would be crossing the border and selling my product in Canada. And the crime rate was lower and the streets less dangerous there. In western New York, the crime rate was so high there was a good chance that I would get robbed navigating through the inner city unless I had some form of security. The main purpose I had for pursuing a music career was to have a positive influence on people while still maintaining my own authenticity.

One night a friend and I set out to sell some CDs. I had an Astro Van with some twenty-inch chrome rims. It also had a serious sound system with subwoofers under the back seat. I went to a vending machine to get some change so that I could wash my van. We had the van looking so clean. The rims were looking so good we could almost see our faces in them. The second after we pulled off to head downtown it was evident that people noticed how shiny the rims were. When it comes to being influential, a great presentation speaks volumes.

One night I was outside a nightclub selling my project. There were so many people purchasing a copy! I was having such a great night and was so thankful for the way things went. Then about five ladies walked by me as they came out of the nightclub. They looked me up and down, staring as they walked by. Two of them began to laugh really loudly while pointing directly at me. A group of people turned and looked at them. One of the ladies almost fell because she was most likely drunk and trying to walk in high heels. One of the ladies stopped and shook her head as she looked me up and down. "I saw you in four cities in the last month selling music." Then she began to yell each city out loud while her girlfriends laughed. To be honest, this did not discourage me. It was actually a compliment and an encouragement even though they did not mean it in a good way. I turned to them, squared my shoulders, and lifted my chin. I looked at all of them with a joy in my heart that I cannot explain and said, "One day you are going to be forced to listen to my music on the radio, and you will remember the day you met Just Love Isaac." I said it not in a boastful way but with confidence, sending the message that they would regret missing their opportunity to connect with me in a positive way.

A man just leaving the club stopped and stood nearby. He had heard and seen the whole thing. He looked at the women as they were walking away and yelled, "Yah need to grow up and do something with your lives," and laughed. He turned to me and said, "I really respect what you are doing out here. I have heard your name more than once." We talked for a bit, and he purchased a copy of my music project. People will try to knock the wind out of your sails, and this is not a new thing.

Shortly after that little distraction, I sold every copy that I had on me that night. Then my friend and I stood by the van, talking to and encouraging people outside the club who might be having a hard time in life. I talked with people about the pursuit of success and what life should really be about. The energy was great. The owner of the club came outside and smiled in our direction.

Then suddenly, three police cruisers pulled up in front of the club, not far from where I was standing. They put on their black leather gloves as they came closer to me. The club owner yelled at the police, "No, no, no! He is a good guy! You have the wrong person!" At this point the police grabbed me and threw me against my van. People were screaming at the officers, "What are you doing?" My friend, who is a family man and law-abiding citizen, was sitting in the front seat of my van. One of the officers aggressively opened the side door, grabbed my friend out of the van by his shirt, and threw him against the van as well. People in front of the club were still screaming at the officers to stop. One officer threatened to arrest the ones expressing their disapprovals of the officers' behavior.

As one of the officers frisked me in every place on my body, I very calmly asked, "Why are you treating me this way? Why are you treating me like a common criminal?"

"Shut up your mouth, and just go with it," was his response.

My frustration turned into anger. I knew that there was a very good chance my life was going to change. Growing up in western New York, I had seen many citizens experience so much wrong by authorities. As a kid growing up, I was influenced by the culture to classify every man in a blue uniform with a gun and a badge as a pig. I saw many cops do so many crooked things while I grew up in the projects. Most people never saw the police in my hood back in western New York as good people, but more as a government-appointed gang.

Now there I was, in another country, in a situation much worse than I expected. These men with a gun and badge were supposed to protect me and help me. To be completely honest, the way he grabbed me and threw me against the van while I watched another cop grab my friend out of the front seat made me not only frustrated and angry but also confused as to why this was happening. After he frisked me, I turned around and asked him again, "Why are you doing this?" He then walked into my personal space and started bumping me. This police officer was actually intentionally trying to provoke me in front of everyone standing outside the club.

People continued to yell at him, and he continued to threaten those in the crowd. He started pushing me and taunting me, "You think you're tough? Let's go right now." He backed me up until I was almost against the building beside the club. In my mind I saw a flash of me cracking him in the face with my fist as hard as I could multiple times. In my mind's eye I saw him crashing to the ground after my fist connected with his face. This was happening at the same time people were screaming, "Leave him alone," over and over.

As I was battling in my thoughts, I prayed softly to myself because if I had acted on them, it could cost me my life and the officer's. I have been involved in fighting disciplines since the age of six, so I have learned things through the years that can take multiple people out almost simultaneously. He was relentless in his pursuit to provoke me to retaliate in some way. Bumping me, pushing me, threatening me, and calling me names I am not willing to utter. Someone yelled, "Hit the stupid pig in the face, Mitchell!"

There are times when people will try to influence you to do things that are easy. However, the consequences for the action can be hard. We can have thoughts of temptations during circumstances, but whenever there is something—a circumstance—that significantly changes our emotional states, we really need to consider what we are feeling. This involves critical thinking. Could I have punched this man in the throat and taken his gun within seconds? Most likely yes. Could there have been a bloodbath on that block that would have been remembered for years to come? Yes most likely. I had to ask myself, "Is this how I want to be remembered?" I cannot allow someone else's influence to divert or intercept the fullness of capturing the legacy that I desire.

This police officer was acting like an untamed beast. But I began to look in his eyes without hearing him, and I saw him as a young boy, who was most likely abused, bullied, or abandoned. Something in this man's life caused him to have these maladaptive patterns before taking on the position of authority. He was a human being with thoughts and feelings and, based on his actions, the intent to do me harm in some way. He had a perception of me as well, provoked by some reason unknown to me.

CHAPTER 6

Take Action

I TOOK A DEEP BREATH, went into a trance-like state, and blocked out everyone there. I dissociated myself from the incident. Everyone was talking to me, including the cop standing in front of me. However, there became a point when I did not hear anyone. I blocked out all distractions, which means that I stopped hearing the influence of the crowd and the taunting of the officer. In my own mind I began to focus on my assignment, which is ultimately to influence others to be the best that they could be in life.

There are those who would consider how I handled this situation heroic or brave. And there are others who may see my approach as passive and cowardly. I believe that at times we need to look deeper into things. Yet we need to keep it simple according to our values. Everyone's values about things vary. I believe it is cowardly to listen to the influence of others at the expense of abandoning our own values. I also believe it takes a person with backbone to be aggressive in staying focused in the process of maintaining the path that leads to the fulfilling of his or her destiny. Despite the opposition, adversity, rejection, and challenges that we encounter.

I looked around and saw the cherry flashing and the people watching. I zoned out and saw myself standing amid what could be something chaotic, or something I could later speak from in a place of being victorious. I felt a peace that I could not comprehend as I meditated on things that correlated with my values. It was then that there was a deescalating of not only me but the officer and the crowd. The officer took a step back and tilted his head to the side. He looked around at the crowd and then back at me. After everything that had happened, I believe he realized his tactics to provoke me into making a bad choice had failed because he asked me, "Do you have any ID"? This question, I believe, is effective for many reasons. It would have been a good idea to ask for my ID at the very beginning. I slid my hand in my pocket without losing eye contact with him and handed him my driver's license, ownership, and insurance. He took my identification and walked through the crowd to his cruiser. I watched him as he sat in the front seat and typed my name into the computer. I then watched his body language as he leaned back, acknowledging his apparent mistake. I could see him looking at the monitor (computer screen) in his car, biting his bottom lip and shaking his head. What he read was that I am high profile, the many contributions I made to the community, and that I was a law-abiding citizen. He got out of the cruiser and walked back to me. He handed me my driver's license, saying, "I'm just doing my job."

I reminded him of what had just happened. "You walk up to me, grab me and my friend, and drag us around like common criminals without just cause."

He responded, "What were you doing by the vending machine?"

"What are you talking about? When I washed my van before coming here?"

Someone allegedly watched me wash my van and called the police on me, saying a black man was stealing from a vending machine and vandalizing. How could someone assume that I was stealing from a machine and destroying property? Even worse, how could the police just grab my friend and me without questioning us first? Once again this shows how the power of influence can be a deadly thing. This police officer was convinced that I was vandalizing and stealing, and I fit the description. The crazy thing is at the time, I was volunteering with a couple of agencies to help youth stay off the streets and out of a life of crime.

The police returned to their cruisers as if nothing happened. No apology, no remorse, no compassion.

I thought about taking some form of legal action after what I had gone through. I set up a meeting with the chief of police with the hope that there would be some sort of internal investigation and accountability for the officers who abused their positions of power. I kept telling myself that all police were not crooked and that the chief of police would follow up. I was given information by an anonymous source that there would be no actual investigation.

About a month later, I made my way to the station. As I walked through the building, I was not treated the greatest. I was given dirty looks by those who were on duty. At this point I began to get angry again. I believe that the gun and badge were triggers, taking me back to the incident. I walked into the chief of police's office and sat down, gnashing my teeth after he asked me to grab a seat in front of his desk. I thought about how it took so long for me to get an appointment to see him; I thought about previous incidents that involved police harassment. He left the room and had me waiting for a while. I had a strong feeling that there were cameras in his office. I felt like I was being watched. The chief wanted me to make a stupid move, like perhaps look through his files or go in his desk. So out of frustration, I decided to put my feet up on his desk to give them something to look at on their hidden cameras.

And about thirty seconds after I did, he came back into the office. He smacked my feet off the desk. "Get your feet off my desk, Mitchell!" He made his way around and sat down. He pulled out some papers and tapped them together on his desk.

I said very calmly, "You need to get a leash on your boys. They are out of control."

"Listen, I know who you are, Mitchell. I will have an internal investigation, and you will be contacted after it is completed."

I made my way out of the office feeling a small sense of hope, though it was tainted by the influence of what I was told by the anonymous source. After about a week I started noticing things, such as a police cruiser sitting outside my house. I also noticed that every time I or anyone in my house went out and took a vehicle, a cruiser followed behind for several blocks. There were also times when I was pulled over though I had not committed any traffic violations. Word got back to me that a couple of officers came by the club and talked to the owner. They warned him that if he said one word about what happened to me in in front of his club that night he would be shut down.

I got a letter every week or two about the investigation. Based on the letters, there seemed to be no progress. Eventually I received a letter stating that the investigation was over, and nothing would be done about how my friend and I were treated.

As time went on, it seemed that the situation grew worse. I continued to get pulled over and questioned even after the investigation was over. I was starting to become so discouraged and felt like doing something extreme to have breathing room. This went on for at least a couple of years.

One night I went out with my son to grab a pizza at a local restaurant. We were laughing and having a great time talking about life and waiting for our order. When the pizza was done, we headed out to the car with our order. A delicious pizza with extra everything on it. My son was just little at the time and was excited to go home and enjoy what we ordered. When we crossed the street, I noticed a cruiser sitting at the lights. I did not get a good feeling as I headed to my car. I played it off, smiling and talking to my son as if I was not bothered or worried. But my heart started to pound because I had a gut feeling that there was going to be some sort of trouble. I sat in the car and checked my rearview mirror. The cruiser seemed to have vanished. I continued to talk with my son as we pulled out and headed home to eat.

Then as soon as I turned down the dark side street that led to my house, I saw the police cherry flashing. The weird thing was that there was not a lot of sound coming from the siren. I checked my rearview again as the cruiser sat idle for about two minutes. The police officer made his way to my car and asked me for my license and insurance. I asked him why I was pulled over. I had my mother on speakerphone at the time of the incident. The officer responded with, "I am not going to talk to you until after you hang up the phone." I asked him for his badge number. He refused to give it to me. So I reached slowly into the glove compartment and grabbed my license and insurance. I handed it to him and again asked why I had been pulled over. He responded, "Your kind needs to be in jail."

I could not believe my ears. He looked at me as if I was an animal. I shook my head without losing eye contact with him. I thought maybe I had not heard him correctly. I responded, "I am sorry. What did you just say?"

He looked me in my eyes with such anger and hate. "You heard me. You and your kind need to be in jail. All of you need to be locked up. You and your kind do not deserve to be out in society." He flashed his light into the back seat and my son's face. My son became increasingly anxious as he kept shining the light in his face. I asked the officer to please stop, but he continued as my son put both his hands in the air, trying to hide his face from the light.

I said, "Please stop this. You are scaring my son." The officer walked back to his cruiser with my ID. I turned around and looked at my son, who was confused and kept looking around in the back seat. I checked my rearview and then my side mirror, going back and forth between mirrors. I looked back at my son with a fake smile on my face and told him that we were going to enjoy the pizza when we got home. "Can you smell it, big man?" He got a half smile on his face. My son was so smart that he picked up that something was wrong.

The officer eventually made his way back to my car. He handed me my driver's license and insurance, and then said, "You are lucky I don't arrest you right now."

"Arrest me for what?" He reached into the car and tossed me a ticket for signing my ownership in pencil. I saw flashes of past incidents in which my rights as a citizen were violated. It felt like I was in a movie from the 1960s dealing with racial discrimination. As he made his way back to his cruiser, I looked up. I sat in my car thinking about everything that was said. Out of frustration I decided to get out of my car. This was not the greatest choice according to civilian protocol. I began walking toward the officer as the cherry flashed on my face looking up at the dark sky on a street with little light.

CHAPTER 7

Don't Be Afraid

MANY THOUGHTS RAN THROUGH MY mind after I took the initiative to open my door and head in the direction of this man with a gun and badge. I had flashes of every incident in the past that involved my interaction with members of the police force. As I got closer to him, he must have felt my energy or heard my steps walking behind him. He looked over his shoulder as I approached him in the distance. He spun around and grabbed his gun, stumbling backwards a few steps. I did not lose a stride. As I walked toward him, I made direct eye contact with him, not even a blink. I kept thinking about all the things that he said to me out of his ignorance.

He yelled at me, "Get back in your car!" His voice was shaky, indicating that anything could happen at that point. He looked like he was ready to pull his gun out any second. He popped the holster as I took a couple more steps forward. I looked at him up and down. He yelled, "I said get back in your car." When I looked him in the eyes this time, I could see panic. His legs were shaking so hard that

I thought he was just joking with me. It looked like his knees were almost knocking together.

I thought, *This is not a good situation for either of us*. When I think back, I can only imagine how I must have looked on that dark street with the cruiser's lights flashing on my face. But I just stood there, looking at him without even blinking. It felt like a scene from a movie. However, I knew by the way he was clenching his gun that this was far from a film. I was so frustrated at that I felt I had nothing to lose. In reality, I had everything to lose, including my life. I told him, "I'm not afraid of you just because you have a gun and a badge. I am not afraid of you. I just want you to know." Then I asked him a familiar question: "Why are you doing this to me? I work to keep kids off the streets. We're on the same team, fighting for our youth."

He yelled over my voice, still clenching his gun at his side, his knees knocking, wild-eyed and unpredictable. "Yeah, right! I know what you are about. Like I said before, you are lucky you are not in jail right now. Now get back in your car like I said."

I did not move, not out of defiance, but more out of wanting this man to understand that I was not a threat, and I was telling the truth. But there seemed to be no reasoning with this man, who was convinced that "my kind" should be locked up. After a few moments of a stare down, I took a few steps backward, turned, and walked back to my car. When I opened my car door and looked inside, my son was leaning forward, trying to see if I was okay. He was so little at the time and was probably still a little confused as to what was going on. I reassured him that everything was okay, and we were going home.

Before I even started my car, the police officer put the pedal to the metal, and spun his cruiser around, doing a U turn and driving on the sidewalk for a moment. He screeched his tires so loudly that the neighbors must have heard him. I very calmly started my car and drove home; fortunately my house was right around the corner.

I began to pace once I got home. I felt a sense of hopelessness, anger, frustration, and isolation. Then my creativity began to kick in. This was when I really had to revisit my values before deciding to follow through with a plan. I had all these feelings, and yet I did not feel afraid. I felt like fighting back, but I did not know how to take this one on.

The first thing that I did was go to my son's room and talk to him about what happened. He looked up at me and said that he and his friends were going to plan to beat up the police. I understood that how I responded to him in this situation would not be just with my words but with my actions, and it would make a huge difference in my son's life. So I immediately sat down and began to explain that not all police officers were bad, and that the police are supposed to protect and help us. He asked, "Then why was the policeman so mean to you, Daddy? And why did he keep putting the light in my face? I was scared, Daddy." I explained to him that this policeman was one of the stinky bad ones.

As I talked with him, my phone rang continuously because family was aware that something serious was going on with me. I cannot lie. Thoughts of committing the most violent acts of revenge battled in my mind with the power of choice. I believe moments like the one I was experiencing have the potential to define who we are. One of my values is to admit the truth and live by it to the best of my ability. I humbled myself and got to my knees that night to pray for answers, for direction. I went to sleep in peace, and my hope was restored without any actual sign of changes.

The next day I received a call from media asking what was new in my life. I have been blessed with great opportunities and have developed solid relationships with media personnel after doing many interviews about sports and entertainment for television, radio, and newspapers. I was immediately told by someone immensely powerful in media that they needed to meet with me. I believe that someone in my family must have informed them about the past incidents. I ended up walking into the police station for an unscheduled meeting and straight into the chief's office. I sat down and did not have to say a word regarding what happened. Someone from the media spoke on my behalf. The police chief was not allowed to talk to me directly without my consent. The chief apologized to me about what happened. This was the first time anyone with a gun and badge had done so. Come to find out, the officer who pulled me over was out of district, which meant that he should not have been in the area.

So many things could have happened in that situation, regardless of who this man with the gun and badge was. The situation evolved into something productive because I try to look at every possible dynamic in a situation. Despite how things appear, there is something great and wonderful to be discovered. As a public figure, I have learned that there are media personnel who are compassionate and insightful critical thinkers who truly care about people.

After the apology, my eyes began to fill up as I realized that my prayer was answered. The targeting would finally cease, or there would be a story that would make headlines. And the police force definitely did not want that to happen. In turn, as a top-40 radio recording artist, any publicity is good publicity if done without the expense of abandoning our values. There will be times when you experience adversity or opposition when you are making choices in life. If they run in line with your values, do not be afraid. Do not allow fear to cause you to make irrational decisions. Think, pray, meditate, and visualize the best outcome, even if it seems impossible for the circumstances to change at first. This can make the difference in not only success or failure but in life and death.

We are given the opportunity through birthright to navigate with an optimistic mindset. No one can stop you from seeing the good in every situation. And no one can stop you from pursuing the destiny that you desire. Do not give up on your dreams, and do not be afraid. You have access to knowledge that will build your capacity and propel you into your desired destiny if you make the time for yourself. When you exercise, cook, clean, drive, my advice is to play motivational material so that your mind is filled with things that will override the negativity you have faced or will face. Material that causes you to visualize the fulfillment of a great life. Say aloud, "I am courageous. I am successful. I am unstoppable. I am loved, and I love myself. My future is bright." Repeat this declaration ten times, and watch how your emotional state shifts for the better. You begin to feed your unconscious mind, and when what you declare becomes part of your inner voice, you will see change; you will see great manifestations. What you think of yourself is who you really are. Think good things about yourself even when no one else does. Say good things about yourself even when no one else does.

I knew that along with me speaking good things over myself that I would tap into my unconscious mind and do things without thinking about it. I knew that I had to forgive what was done to me to advance in life. It has been proven that unforgiveness can cause sickness and disease. It can also block positive things from happening for us.

I decided to go for a jog in the city one day. A police cruiser came up and was driving beside me. The officer kept looking over at me as I ran. I thought, *This can be an opportunity to express what I am feeling inside*. We kept looking at each other, back and forth. Finally it came to a stop at a red light. Cars that were driving by even began to slow down to watch our nonverbal interaction.

Fear from the past can have a crippling effect in our current states, and it can paralyze us from moving forward. Some belief systems have taught us through cultural conformity that reconciliation shows weakness. I believe it shows just the opposite. When someone has the skills to implement conflict resolution, it shows intelligence and strength. I cannot lie. When I am in fight mode in any aspect of my life, my walk changes, my facial expressions shift, and I become focused on not only winning but on finding understanding.

I finally made the decision to make the first move, so I headed toward the police car. The officer noticed me coming in his direction. As I walked toward him, I admit that I saw some flashes in my mind from past altercations involving police officers. I was dripping with sweat and wore jogging pants and a black hood. I kept thinking, *Things need to change*. He leaned in my direction as I got closer. My face was stone cold because this was a serious moment for me. I looked inside the cruiser, and we made eye contact as he leaned in my direction. I thought about him pulling out his revolver, as police officers had done in the past. I then began think, *I am not afraid*. I leaned into the car, still holding eye contact.

CHAPTER 8

We Are Human

I LEANED IN ON THE passenger side of the cruiser. The officer then popped the question, "May I help you?"

I responded, "Yeah, I want to give you my card." I know that it is prohibited for law enforcement to take any items from civilians at any time, but for some reason he took my card. I explained that my gym was five miles from where we were standing. I invited him to come to one of my boxing classes and gave the officer free admission for a week. He smiled and thanked me. He said that he would like to join eventually. He had heard my name before and was a boxing fan. He mentioned that he would like to pass my contact information on. I thanked him and continued with my jog. Once again I noticed all the people who were staring in our direction.

I felt like a weight had been lifted after I took the first step in attempting to bring some sense of reconciliation. Feelings are not wrong. However, what we do with our feelings make a difference.

47

One of the greatest heavyweights of all time had a trainer, who made the profound statement, "The hero and the coward, they both feel the same, it's what they do that makes them different." In my opinion, it is one's character that reveals who one really is.

Fear is only a thought. I believe we can make rational decisions while overcoming fear. We are human, but we do not have to live in fear. Whenever you are put in a situation where fear challenges you, it's a good exercise to close your eyes and visualize and meditate on the opposite of what you are afraid of. After I gave the officer my card and invited him to the gym, every time I saw a police car, my fear of being set up, harassed, or even brutalized diminished.

About a month later, I was driving to the gym and running late for an appointment. I went to make a left-hand turn and ended up pulling right in front of a police cruiser. I checked my rearview mirror and noticed that the cop was constantly looking down, which indicated that he was looking at his keyboard or a computer monitor. I looked up a few more times in my side mirror and noticed that the cherry began to flash. It was then I remembered that the sticker on my license plate had expired. I knew that I should have taken care of it. It was my fault for not making this matter a priority.

The officer pulled me over and asked for my identification. It clicked that I had left the house in a rush and without my wallet. He asked if I wanted to make sure that everyone knew that I was going to be a little late for the class. The officer and I walked into the gym together. He said he was going to let the driving without a proper ID ticket go if I brought it to the station within forty-eight hours. He was very polite and very fair and respectful. I received a small ticket, but it could have been much worse. He looked around the gym and seemed impressed with the atmosphere. He turned to me in front of a few clients, looked me directly in the eyes, and said, "Not long ago I saw this guy jogging down the street, and he invited me to the gym. I believe that it was you!"

I smiled and replied, "Yes, that was me." The officer said he really appreciated that I took the time to invite him. This really set things into perspective for me. I eventually began to train some officers through my boxing program.

Years went by, and I developed a good rapport with some of the men and women who served and protected. So I had the opportunity to meet a few good people. Some were highly ranked in the force and assured me that if I ever had any problems with any officer to inform them, and they would have my back. Hearing about everyday family stuff, sharing back and forth caused me to see that we are all human. Hearing a man talk about his wife and kids and the great time they had at the fun park or playing in the backyard by the pool made them human. The truth of the matter is that some police officers may act like animals, and some citizens may do the same. However, we are all human, and it is our character that defines us.

While writing this book, I heard a story about a police officer restraining a man who had just committed a crime. Another man walked up behind the officer and shot him in the back of the head. The officer had a wife, children, and an extended family. It was said that he was a good person who had morals and cared about people. These types of incidents are just as wrong as police brutality. I have the understanding that there is a degree of cultural conformity within those who serve in the force. Assertiveness should be respected if it lines up with values that reflect serving and protecting. But the systemic issues that exist have many confounding factors. Humans are prone to be unconsciously biased at times. Specially skilled, ethnically diverse individuals should be appointed to revise and improve the requirements pertaining to qualification for the police psychological exam. There should be an increased number of stages involving psychological analysis before someone receives a gun and badge. I also believe that it should be mandatory for every officer to undergo random checks (being monitored) throughout his or her entire time serving in the force.

A gun, a badge, and a uniform do not make a man or woman immune to poor choices. I believe society's moral decline and other social issues are what can infect and affect the choices of someone serving in the force. Making decisions while being constantly bombarded with extremely stressful situations without accountability from those outside the force can be destructive. We must take the proper approach to see progress for the good of both civilians and law enforcement. Before things get worse.

We cannot ignore how the system has failed us tremendously. In my opinion, the bigger issue within the police force is not racism. The root of some of the concerns stems from ignorance. In my limited understanding, our educational system lacks the exploration, appreciation, and information about the historical backgrounds and contributions made to society by every race, creed, and culture. I learned many things about European history through the educational system. I remember the moment that I became aware of the true historical background of contributions made by Afrocentric descendants pertaining to inventions, discoveries, positive impacts, and so on. The absence of this information creates an incorrect perspective, subconsciously creating stigmas and general outlooks that are twisted or erroneous.

How can you appreciate me as an individual if there are negative projections superimposed through media, television, and the internet? My history consists of more than cotton pickers, hustlers, drug dealers, slaves, and criminals. We are scientists, inventors, activists, doctors, lawyers, innovators, technological geniuses, prominent figures, and much more. I had to do my own research outside school because it is not taught within their four walls as it should be. Nor is true history taught within family homes. This is the root of many dysfunctional mindsets pertaining to racial discrimination. How can we function in and navigate through society, in the workforce, or in any corporate setting without corrupt or perverse perceptions of people if we are ignorant to each other's unique potentials or achievements?

I believe that there are devils in every race. Incorrect information can create the element of fear, and in turn, this can cause people to make choices based on someone's complexion or race. If our unconscious states have been injected with the poison of discrimination or continuous ignorance, we will attract experiences that will feed what is alive within us. I have learned to search for the good in every person I meet, even if I have heard negative things about the person. If we have the intent to find out something about a person, good or bad, we often see a manifestation of what it is we are looking for.

I pulled into a gas station and asked the man working there if he could give me $40 of gas. He rolled his eyes and began swearing under his breath. I heard him dropping the F bomb while rolling his eyes at me. He slammed the hose in the tank hole and continued looking at me, swearing under his breath. He checked my oil and slammed my hood as hard as he could. All type of thoughts crossed my mind about his behavior. *Was he a racist? Was he having a bad day? Did I unknowingly do something in the past to offend him?* He seemed so negative. And in my mind I began to get ticked for how he was acting. I instantly had thoughts of telling him off for how he slammed the hood of my car and the obscene things directed at me that he uttered under his breath.

Not to be spooky, but I closed my eyes for a second and heard a suggestive thought, *Ask him if he is okay.* My whole agenda changed as I began to question why someone would act this way. The root of the issue was not his behavior. The deeper issue was what was going on in his mind to cause him to behave the way he was.

I am aware that soft words can defuse anger at times. So I got out of my car and walked up to him as he was still pumping my gas. I asked, "Are you okay? Is everything all right?

He rolled his eyes and asked, "Why? Why do you care?" as he swore under his breath.

"It looks like you are having a hard time with something. Is there anything I can do to help you?"

His facial expressions began to change. He no longer looked angry. He looked down and then back up at me. I could see the pain in his face. "My mother died yesterday." My eyes immediately filled with tears as this man began to speak openly about his mom.

I stayed there at the gas station with him for about a half an hour, trying to console him. We exchanged contact information before I left. I noticed that he was smiling and telling me stories about some of his life experiences. Something seemed different about him in a special way. I have worked with people who have mental issues, and it came out that he had been battling autism as well. I ended up taking him out with a mutual friend who specializes in helping people with these challenges. We went out to eat, and my friend and I had a great time sharing and encouraging him. I ended up seeing this man pop up in different places all over the city. I wondered, *What if I had focused on what was in front of me? What if I did not search out the good in this person? What if I had let my emotions rule my decisions? I would have never had the experience of meeting someone and making a positive impact on his life.*

What I learned through this experience was that we never know what someone may be going through. This awareness has caused me to avoid being myopic and instead attempt to search for the good in everyone I have contact with. We are human, and there is always something good to be discovered if we are willing to search. If our purposes are greater than ourselves, it will cause a selflessness in our character and in our nature. Purpose will transport us into new places. It is the vehicle of greatness.

CHAPTER 9

Who Do You Think You Are?

TO PRODUCE A DIAMOND IT takes thousands of years of heat and pressure. This process creates something incredibly beautiful. What I find incredibly significant about this precious jewel is the fact that it is transparent. You can see right through it. Nothing is hidden within it. Imitation diamonds are not truly authentic, but the ones that are real are valuable. After all the disappointments you have experienced, please understand that it is not the worst thing that can happen if you have experienced rejection, betrayal, envy, hatred, or any other negative projections or attitudes from others.

Experiencing things like this can ultimately be used as an agent to thrust you into a life of great success and happiness—if you keep the right attitude. I believe that it is a privilege to be in a place of influence in someone else's life, especially in a positive way. For instance, rejection can be one of the most painful experiences to go through. But it can also be one of the greatest agents toward your success and happiness. Rejection can cause a person to take on the element of fear, and it can affect the decisions the individual makes. There is danger in this because opportunities can be missed if we operate by fear. Understand rejection as a super-great announcement that does not always reflect who we are, but it can also reveal who the person is who has rejected you. Understand there is a possibility that you are growing internally, even if you do not see it. Hence, the person who rejected you has fulfilled his or her purpose in your life for the time connected to you.

Then there are people who stay connected to you because of their own insecurities. One way to identify this way of thinking is to ask yourself these questions: Are the people in my life uplifting to me? Am I continuously being put down in some way, or am I consistently being controlled, manipulated, or pressured to do things that I might not want to? Do the things that I feel uncomfortable with contribute toward my advancement?

You must understand that people will always have opinions of you, especially bullies. I may have made this statement in the past, and I can guarantee that I will repeat in the future: "Never allow someone to hold you hostage by their opinion of you. It is not fair to you or the people you are connected to. You are unique, you have greatness locked inside you, and no one will steal the power that lives in you. It is time for you to begin to think about what you like to do that involves helping other people in some way. The greatness that is inside you will not be unlocked any other way." I learned that being selfish did not make me happy. It is only when I give that I find a sense of fulfillment and happiness. Self-centered people will go to great lengths to have self-fulfillment, even at the expense of hurting others. What is it that makes you happy and involves helping other people, at least in some sense?

Be aware that a person who puts you down has something inside that he or she is trying to fulfill. Taking control of someone else s life is only a temporary sense of satisfaction. Therefore, the bully will seek out and target someone repeatedly and eventually escalate if it is not dealt with by the person being targeted or by someone who intervenes to help. There is help for you today. It is time to tap into what you have access to. Winning, losing, success, and failure takes place in the mind before it takes place externally. If we are focusing on the negative things that someone says about us, we will miss our advancements. We need to focus on good things by exercising visualization of past goals, present goals, and every future goal that is positive.

There also needs to be insight about what could cause us to delay progress by exposing these things. The first so-called negative thing that we talked about with the potential to come from some people is rejection. When someone points something out in you, it is often because what they are pointing out is alive in him or her. Positive or negative, good or bad. That goes the same for you reading this book, my friend. Do you have the capability of looking for the good in someone, even if the person gets under your skin? Can you search for every good quality in a person, the person who bugs you most? Something good is in them, even if you cannot see it right away. Sometimes it may take a little more time to identify what it is, but everyone has at least one good quality in their character to be discovered. If I cannot recognize at least one good quality in someone who annoys, frustrates, or irritates me, then I believe without a doubt that I have a problem.

To be honest, I have had to learn how to exercise this way of thinking, and it was not easy. However, I have worked with youth for many years, and I have also learned that this principle should be applicable toward adults as well. I have had the great opportunity of entering facilities where people have been incarcerated for some of the hardest crimes in the country. I would show up in the morning at nine o'clock and stay all day. I had access into what is known as the belly of the beast. I would be behind bars in jails/prisons and speak to the inmates for the day. I have spoken to groups and have had one-on-one sessions as well, where I have locked individuals into their visions and purposes. This was volunteer work that I have done for years. I have found that many people have misconceptions of the nature of anyone who happens to be in prison or in jail. Every case is different as far as the reason for the incarceration, but I believe we should look at them as people. Some people who have made bad choices in life, and some who were at the wrong place at the wrong time. There are individuals who have been incarcerated for many years, attended sessions of my Life, Vision, and Purpose Program (Motivational Fire), and their lives were changed completely because of their new awareness of the greatness that lives within them. I have run into people in society who now have established businesses, a healthy family environment, and many other transitions into better lives. It is not fair to look at someone and judge him or her, or have a preconceived notion about someone without hearing the whole story about the person's life or situation.

An ongoing problem with social media, or any other type of social interaction, is when people hear one side of the story and not the whole story. This deletes the authentic parts of relationships because people develop an unconsciously biased mindset. This happens often with social media, and as a result, cyberbullying is often extremely hard to combat. There is the possibility of hearing only one side of someone's story, that of someone who is motivated by the intention of bullying. The dangerous thing about this type of interaction is the fact that there can be thousands or even millions who witness it. In many cases, people will not step in to help someone being victimized or fight against this type of behavior. I have made a conscious decision to become active in fighting against bullying.

I was dating a woman who had an uncle with Down syndrome. He used to often tap his comb on his hand while making noises in his throat. He had such a good heart and was loved by the family. My girlfriend was really concerned about him because his behavior had been off for months. She found out some young punks on the bus made fun of him and other people who were mentally challenged on the city bus he took home from school every day. They would tell her uncle and the others to move to the front or the back. She was told the bullies were laughing loudly and making rude comments to them; some were even degrading. No one was speaking up for the ones being bullied. The bus driver was intimidated by the bullies to the point that he said nothing in response to their behaviors.

I had no idea who these dudes were. I knew nothing about them except their poor choice to bully innocent people. I thought, *I have to do something about it, even if no one else will.* So I asked what the bus route was and what time he got on to come home from school. After gathering this information, I never said another word. I waited a couple more days, hoping that my then-girlfriend would forget I asked. Then one day I drove my car and parked it on a side street near where to bus route would travel. I walked about a mile toward the beginning of the route. I must admit that with every step I took toward where the bus would pass, I got angrier just thinking about what these mentally challenged people were going through. I must be honest. I was having so many thoughts about what I wanted to inflict on these jerks. Let us not forget that I had the killer instinct of a fighter in me at the time. It would not matter to me how big these guys were or even how many there were. At the time, I just wanted justice at any cost.

I looked into the distance and saw a bus coming in my direction. So many thoughts rushed through my mind as I walked to the bus stop and waited to get on. The noise of the bus got louder as it approached closer and closer. I had not taken the bus in a while, so before getting on, I asked someone how much it cost. I had the exact change prepared before getting on. I had my Yankee hat pulled down just above my eyes, which made me somewhat unrecognizable to anyone who may have known me from boxing. As I walked down the aisle toward the back of the bus, I noticed that my girlfriend's uncle was sitting there quietly. At least a few other mentally challenged individuals were seated close to him around the center of the bus. I sat down and listened for anything that seemed to fit the stories that I heard from my girlfriend.

Everything seemed fine as we continued on the scheduled route. Then I suddenly heard an outburst of laughter coming from some of the seats in front of me on the other side. I listened attentively and began to pick up what was being said. These college students were up to no good as they continued to escalate their bullying tactics. One of them was so loud when he told one of the mentally challenged students to leave his seat and sit in the back for no apparent reason, except to order him around. The other students continued to laugh as the mentally challenged student turned around in his seat and looked at the one giving him demands. This mentally challenged student got out of his seat and moved to the back, following the bully's orders. As he walked toward me, he spoke to himself; he had a speech impediment. I stood up and placed my hand gently on his left shoulder. I softly told him to go back to his seat. I could still hear the laughter from the other students, but they could not see me from where I was standing.

After placing my hand on his shoulder and guiding him back to his original seat, I turned around and faced those who were laughing and the bully who had ordered him to change seats. I felt the fire within me begin to blaze as I gnashed my teeth and clenched my fist. I am not going to lie. At this point my thoughts and feelings about this situation were troubling. In truth, I wanted to really hurt everyone involved in bothering these innocent students who were unable to defend themselves. Images that involved me doing really bad things to hurt them rapidly passed through my mind as I looked at them in anger and fury. Then I asked, "Who do you think you are? And what do you think that you are doing?" This was a loaded question to them, but at the time I did not recognize what I was really asking them. I admit that I also threatened them with things I am not able to write about in this book. I was not mature in my fight against these bullies and helping others to think fearlessly. But I have grown in this area since this incident. I made them apologize to the students who were mentally challenged. Each of them followed through easily and quickly. Before leaving I left them with the promise that if I heard anything else about their repeated behavior I would return to the bus for a reason that they would regret.

As I walked down the aisle, I looked to my left at the bus driver. He turned to me and said, "Thank you so much." I then looked back again at the guys who had projected fear on those who were vulnerable and precious in my eyes and gave them a five-second glare. They just looked down or out the window. As I moved down the stairs, all the students cheered very loudly and clapped their hands. Even people who were not involved but witnessed what happened celebrated as well. After leaving the bus, I turned toward the side window and stared some more. The students just looked away. The students who experienced the bullying talked among themselves, smiling and enjoying the ride.

One significant part of the engagement and interaction for me was when I asked them, "Who do you think you are, and what do you think you are doing?" I believe the guys who were bullying had no understanding of their true purposes in life. If I had the opportunity to talk to them again, I would not be so quick to threaten them. I would simply say to them, "You are better than this," and explain to them why.

CHAPTER 10

You Are Valuable

WITHOUT A DOUBT, DISCRIMINATION BASED on pigmentation still exists. I know this from firsthand experience. I believe that racism is a form of bullying. This can be a touchy subject for some people, however. It is something that happens every day somewhere in the world. When this way of life sticks its ugly head up, I am grateful as in my opinion, it is much worse when it hides and navigates passive-aggressively. Though it can be much harder to detect, all the signs will eventually expose racism, and once that happens, we must be encouraged to cut its ugly head off.

It is obvious that I am not speaking about physically combatting bullying. Once again, we attack bullying by developing internal strength through awareness of our given potentials and putting a plan in place. I must drill this home. This plan involves having a vision with a purposeful goal greater than ourselves. You may hear me repeat more than once that our vision must have something within it that ultimately involves helping someone else. Our perspectives toward other people must have key elements that will propel us to want to move toward a vision that entails helping someone other than ourselves. There are sometimes hidden hindrances with the potential to block the fulfillment of a vibrant and successful vision.

At times we are tribal by nature. However, judging someone by the color of their skin rather than their qualities of characters can be a great blockage in many ways. When I first relocated from an all-black school in western New York to Canada, I was somewhat devastated after I experienced a cultural shock. My mannerisms and how I spoke were different from what people were used to when I arrived in Canada and started attending school. As I sat in the classroom, people deliberately pointed out the different things about me culturally and tried to make fun of my accent. I even sometimes caught the tail end of whispered racist jokes. I felt alienated because I talked differently, acted differently, and looked different than my peers. They would express how different I was with undertones or passive-aggressive messages that made me feel like an outcast during parties, after-school functions or any other social interactions. I did have a degree of popularity from participating in basketball, football, volleyball, wrestling, the drama team, and so on. We went to championships in each sport.

But despite my popularity, I became somewhat of a loner. There was a time when I began to believe that something was wrong with me because I often found myself alone. I became somewhat angry because of the confusion caused by my lack of understanding why I was rejected and misunderstood.

Around this time my parents enrolled me into jujitsu with an instructor named Harold. He had fought in some of the first televised

UFC matches. This is most likely why no one dared try to physically bully me around this time.

Though that helped one area of my life, I believe I subconsciously began to feel somewhat inferior to the other students. When there was history class, I noticed not much was taught about Afrocentric history. I learned in school that my ancestors consisted of cotton pickers and slaves. And as far as what I saw in the media, black people seemed to have a proclivity toward criminal activities. There was no historical background given about the many positive contributions that have been made to society by my North American and African ancestors. I remember sitting through geography class and I felt that when the teacher spoke about the African civilization, he seemed to project that African people were uncivilized savages. There was nothing about the contributions that have been made throughout the world. However, the geography teacher did touch on the natural resources that are found even today on the continent known as the "Cradle of Life."

I had to decide to just accept what was told to me or to do my own research about my true historical background. As I began to discover the many contributions that were made through my ancestors, it produced something in me that could not be hidden. I experienced a paradigm shift on a deeper level. The absence of knowledge about myself blocked me from truly progressing in life in so many areas. Do not get me wrong. I have found that in some secondary schools today there are teachers who will take the time to teach through means of authentic education. The train-to-train communication system, agricultural expert who advise the President, the first self made female millionaire, the coinventor of the personal computer, microphone technology, the improving of blood banks, the gas mask, the first traffic light with 3 commands, NASA engineer, the super soaker, Did you know that these were all African Americans? Countless African Americans throughout history have crossed lines of greatness.

I believe that if people are ignorant of the positive contributions a culture or ethnic group has made to society it can create stigmas and stereotypes. We can unconsciously develop biases towards certain people that, in turn, can cause a person to mistreat, misjudge, and misunderstand someone because of ignorance. This can be another cause of having a bully mentality. Looking at someone and judging the individual by his or her appearance is not fair. We all have done it to some degree because we are humans and live in a society in which many things are based on appearance. Just because a person has a tattoo or multiple tattoos, piercings, a different color hair, or dresses a certain way doesn't mean we should shun or look down on him or her without getting to know the individual's character. People are hurting because they have been treated in negative ways because someone has a view about them based on their appearance. This is not right for so many reasons, yet it happens frequently in our society. The next time you see someone who looks different or dresses different, I encourage you to search for the person's good qualities with no preconceptions. The challenge may be to give someone a chance by accepting the differences, including appearance. Look past what you initially see. Begin to explore the good things about those you come in contact with, without allowing appearance to block you from seeing the good things within them.

As I mentioned earlier, I was angry about the rejection I received throughout school. I was confused because of the pain of feeling like an outcast. However, the anger that I had was not expressed. Rather, it was turned within and caused me to become depressed. At one point in my life I did not have the desire to live anymore. I was medicated by doctors but then turned to self-medicating, using alcohol to lessen the pain of rejection.

You may know someone who has experienced similar things. Or perhaps you can relate to what you are reading. You are not alone. But things are going to get better. The fact that you are reading this book is proof that there is someone with you on your journey, my friend, and it is a great honor for me to be a small part of the greatness contributed toward your life, vision, and purpose. You must know that you are special. You have something that others need, even if you do not see it right now. You may be different from those around you, but do not be discouraged by this. All the things that you have experienced in life—good and bad—have caused you to be the way you are. You are beautiful, strong, talented, and awesome in so many ways. There are times we should take responsibility for the choices that we make. But some things that happened were not your fault, so stop placing the blame on yourself. We must not take our pain or our feelings about our past disappointments out on the people to whom we are connected or who happen to be around us. Sometimes we need to vent or talk to someone who understands to prevent ourselves from hurting others. What has happened to you that made you begin to look down on yourself or someone you are connected to in some way? Your life is valuable, and so are the lives of others. If you regularly find yourself super-annoyed with someone you are connected to and find yourself expressing your annoyance by making the person pay in some way, it could very well be that you lack the skill and motivation to search out the good qualities you do not see, starting within yourself. If you do not see the good qualities of character in yourself, it may be difficult to recognize and celebrate them in others. It is not good for one's health to hate or hurt someone intentionally in anyway just because we do not like something about the person, for example, skin color or appearance. If you are experiencing this, there are people who can help you solve this problem. I believe it would most likely be more difficult to get help if you are the one infected with thought patterns that target people because of the shame that is attached to this activity or the fear of future consequences. It takes tremendous courage to admit this to yourself first, and even more courage to admit it to someone else that you have been a victim of social injustice or have mistreated someone else.

Not to change the subject, but I miss my grandad so much. We would talk for hours. He was soft-spoken, strong, and a solid provider for the whole family. He used to take me to the backyard to look at his garden. There were tomatoes, cucumbers, collard greens, and other fresh vegetables. He showed me how to plant seeds and cultivate them by watering them on a regular basis, creating the right environment for them to grow. At first I would just see soil with nothing but little tags placed to remind where the seeds were planted and what they were. After a while, the plant would grow and the veggies would appear. Some would die early if they were not taken care of properly. And some would grow until ripe and ready to be picked. What Grandad planted was valued by himself, his family, and loved ones.

I would pick a tomato or cucumber, take it into the house, and rinse it off. Grandad would season it with salt, pepper, and some vinegar. He would take some collard greens from the garden and boil them with turkey neck bone for flavor. He made cornbread, black-eyed peas, fried fish, and barbecued chicken. Before we could enjoy the full meal, some of the food we would eat had to be grown. For us to enjoy certain things in life, we must plant good things in the people with whom we are connected, whether we like them or not. Can you see the good in dirt? It might be looked at as a bad thing at times, but it has its value. Not to compare someone to dirt. It is just that something very great can come out of dirt if the right seeds are planted.

Something very precious has been implanted in you: the seeds of vision and purpose in the form of encouraging words. Nothing can stop the good things that are about to happen in your life if you act on what you are aware of today. It's time to think fearlessly about your destiny while recognizing the value found within yourself and those you are connected to.

CHAPTER 11

Vision and Purpose Now

THE ABILITY TO THINK ABOUT or plan the future with imagination or wisdom only exists in the mind until we begin to put things into action. It takes courage to start something when no one else believes or sees the same thing that you do. It takes even more courage to finish it. One thing I have learned is that if we have the expectation of someone always believing and seeing the same vision, it is a great recipe for disappointment. Some people will support you from beginning to end when it comes to helping you fulfill your vision. However, there are people who do not want to see you succeed. It may be based on their own insecurities or fears. So instead of finding their own visions and life purposes, they spend energy trying to stop you from fulfilling yours. It may not be straight up in your face, where you can see it. It could come in the form of undertones or passive-aggressive actions. We must never allow someone to put limitations on us. We can miss out on the best things in life if we do not understand that the impossible can become possible.

How sad is it living life with a constant fear of someone's opinion preventing you from having a vision or a goal? One sign of a person who is controlled by fear or the opinion of someone else is a person who will not act on his or her creative idea. It stays locked up, existing only as a dream or fantasy. Does failure justify sitting and doing nothing just to say we are safe from repeated failures. No way! I will be the first to admit that I have failed time and time again. I have invested a lot of time, money, and resources into things that have crumbled right in front of me. So some people have stopped believing in me. Some people have even made suggestive thoughts that I will never succeed. The truth of the matter is that I refuse to let someone bully me into a mundane state of mind.

The same goes for you, my friend. People may stop believing in you, but you better not stop believing in yourself. When we pursue greatness, another person's doubt or negative words can be an agent for growth and development. It is called resistance, which is something that can build strength. Keep in mind that with most things in life, once growth stops, decay begins. Have you noticed that when someone succeeds, many people will talk about the person, saying things like, "I always knew that she could do it" or "I always knew that he was smart"? They may have said that they believed in you from the beginning, but this may turn out to not be the case. In other words, they may have initially suggested that the person in pursuit of fulfilling a vision or goal would never succeed, while actually visualizing the person's success before giving their negative suggestive thoughts and words of failure. Let me show it to you in another light.

Without attempting to oversimplify the complexities of the human mind, it is my belief that the essence of a thought is an image. It is a visualization of something in the mind. Whenever we think of something, we first see it in our minds. There is great danger yet great beauty in understanding this process. For instance, if a person has received information about your vision or goal, the moment this thought enters the other person's mind, he or she sees it! It is then that the person can accept or reject what you see. It may not appear at first that they see what you see if their words suggest the opposite of what you see. The reason it appears this way is because words have power. However, the moment the initial thought that you have leaves your mouth and others receive it, they can accept it or reject it. What is it that is happening? You have an image in your mind of something that you foresee yourself accomplishing, and you share this image (thought). It is then that whoever is listening can receive your image (thought) and celebrate with you or reject it by conjuring up an image (thought) in his or her mind of you failing, achieving your goal, or fulfilling your vision.

As I mentioned earlier, there is both danger and beauty in words. It is my belief that words form images that will eventually move from an intrinsic state to a becoming what is known as our reality. Hey! You do not believe it? Or are you finding it hard to comprehend what I am saying? All right, watch this. I am about to demonstrate how easy it is to get inside your head. Are you ready for this? Follow along with me. Take seven deep breaths. Then do not think about a red banana. Don't think about a waterfall. Don't think about an airplane flying. Unless you are a vegetable, you visualized every image—thought— that I projected to you.

It can take seconds, minutes, hours, years, or even decades to replace the negative thoughts that are projected to us with another thought that is productive and for our good. Do not allow anyone to bully you in your thought life. When someone tries to inject suggestive words of failure, repel them! How? Simply begin to think the opposite of what someone is saying to you. It may be difficult at times to figure out what that opposite is because of their injection. Words can be an antidote, much like medicine. It is necessary to actually speak the words out loud at times. Do not underestimate the power of the spoken word.

I am from the realm of boxing, and what I love most about the sweet science of boxing is its psychological aspects. Ali said, "I am the … You can finish the thought." Even though he lived in an era when many African Americans had the struggle of civil rights, this man stood up within his own mind and said, "I will not accept anything less than being known as the greatest." He used his vocal cords to declare who he believed he was, even if others did not believe it. There were many people who labeled him as a boisterous, arrogant man. I believe he was just the opposite. Let us not forget arrogance is a false pretense, or thinking of ourselves more highly than we ought to think. However, humility is admitting the truth and living by it. Now I am not saying that everyone is called to profess publicly their visualizations of greatness. This can be dangerous if we are not strong in exercising visualization of success in our thought lives. Once people hear of your vision, they may attack your vision or belief system with their own thoughts of failure and defeat. Can you stand firm in your thought life?

I have fought against the best fighters in the world as I travelled with the national boxing team. I have been to France, Ireland, Africa, England, across Europe, and North and South America. There were people who told me that I would never be a champion. I was sitting in the classroom, and the teacher asked all the other students what we would like to do for a career. There were some who said that they would like to be a fireman, policeman, paramedic, NHL player, or schoolteacher. Everyone was encouraged by the teacher and the other classmates. When the teacher asked me, I said I would like to be a champion boxer. Without hesitation, the teacher looked at me with a big smile on his face and talking out of the side of his mouth said, "It will never happen!" Laughing came from all around me. Laughing came from both sides of the room. One dude even fell off his chair cracking up.

I was somewhat confused by this because I thought everyone was celebrating each other. But apparently except when it was my turn to share. I was somewhat angry and even felt betrayed, especially after hearing the teacher go on and on about how it would never happen. When I asked him, "Why can't it happen for me?" he replied, "You are too much of a thinker and intellectual. You are too soft. You gotta be hard and rugged for the fight game." My heart hit the floor. With all the negative energy surrounding me, it took a few moments for me to bounce back. I looked up and said in a soft voice, "I will do it. I will be a champion one day, even if you do not believe it." To be honest, because of the voices of negativity, I was uncertain if I could really do it.

In an earlier chapter, I mentioned a man, who trained one of the greatest fighters of all time. He said, "There is the hero and the coward. They both feel the same. It's what they do that makes them different." To make a long story short, I ended up making that teacher a liar at least seven times. It was not an easy task, but it happened.

I have learned ways to overcome my fears. One thing that I have devoted myself to doing is lifting myself up by speaking positive words to myself as I jog or even going for a drive in the car by myself. I say things like, "I am going to complete this project. I am great at what I do. I am not alone on my journey. I refuse to settle. I have the best. I am the best. I respect myself. I love me." Or in the morning or at night, I look in the mirror and talk to myself, repeating, "There is nothing impossible for you to accomplish. I am called for greatness. I am chosen for greatness." This may sound and feel a little weird at first. It may even feel like you are bragging. But the truth is you are great. Saying these words in secret to reinforce your purpose is a good thing. Remember words have power. We must never speak negatively over ourselves or allow or accept other people's negative words. It will happen at times, but just be aware, and combat negative words with positive words. Say the opposite of the negative things you hear. Speaking it aloud can shift the atmosphere for the better.

When I had my first fight, I was sixteen years old. It was against a man named David Hook. He was eighteen years old, strong, and a gym rat. Rumor had it that his dad beat him up as a kid. Going into the ring I felt like I was in a dream. Round 1 he came right at me, throwing hook after hook. I had never experienced getting hit like that. His name matched his style of fighting. I lost the first two rounds. He was stronger than me and more experienced. I never went down during the fight, although after getting hit like that, I think I have a rather good idea of what it means to be rocked by a barrage of punches. I never hit the canvas. One thing that I find incredibly significant is despite this loss, I remember to never allow fear to prevent me from pushing forward in life. We must think fearlessly.

CHAPTER 12

Think Fearlessly

WHAT IS THIS THING CALLED fear? There have been many interpretations and definitions given to describe fear, including, "an unpleasant emotion caused by the belief that someone or something is dangerous, likely to cause pain, or a threat."[1] Fear has affected everyone in the human race who has the ability to process potential outcomes of different events or circumstances. It often invades our internal dialogues without restraint or remorse. It can cripple the strongest individuals.

This invisible thing called fear can be so convincing that it can appear to manifest even when it does not exist externally. The words that we speak can often confirm or reveal if this component is part of our internal dialogue. What does this mean exactly? Internal dialogue usually refers to a conversation that takes place that is "inner" and "unspoken." The foundation of my perspective pertaining to the

[1] Lexico, s.v. "fear," accessed February 10, 2021, https://www.lexico.com/en/definition/fear.

element of this thing called fear is that "Fear is only a thought." The essence of fear can appear to be much more complex than what it is. At times it can even have a scent that others can pick up on if it resonates within another person.

There are those who feed off the frequency of fear, propelled to do so by their own dispositions. What happened to that job or line work that you were so excited about going after? The career goals that you spoke so passionately about? The vision, the purpose that you once could visualize for your life? The significant other whom you could see yourself falling in love with forever? The project that you started with such zeal, yet because of circumstances that existed or maybe never actually existed, your hope was overshadowed by the darkness of fear? You may have had an expectation or desire for something to happen, but it may not have turned out exactly the way you or I desired. It is my belief that we are meant to have desires, some of which are healthy, and some of which are not. For instance, having the desire to control someone else's life is not a productive objective. There is a degree of wanting to help someone work through life's difficult situations and to initiate a plan of action, which is somewhat different than just trying to take control of someone's life through intimidation or by force. I have had dreams, goals, and visions shatter right before my eyes and have needed people to pour into me their words of encouragement to activate my hope that may have been lost. So now it is your time to have your hope activated once again.

Let us go back to my first description of fear as being a "thought." I believe that there exists within us all the invisible complexities of the human mind. Throughout the years I have questioned how to describe or define what this thing is that we know of as a thought.

Some believe that it is an idea or opinion produced by thinking suddenly in the mind. But let's look more in depth at this complex process yet define it with simplicity. When information is received and processed in the mind, it is my understanding that it enters through one or all our physical senses—the eyes, ears, skin, mouth, nose, all of which are gateways. Through this process a thought is formed. As I mentioned earlier, I see a thought as simply an image formed in the mind. Hence, we can use all five senses at times. As I stated earlier, I would define a thought as an image. A blind person's realm of perception is formed through four of the senses. And if the ears are functioning, there is a technique known as echolocation. I find it amazing that through the use of touch or clicking of the tongue, tapping a stick, or listening to echoes as the sound bounces off objects in the surroundings, images are formed in the mind. For example, before a person begins to exhibit certain acts of social injustice on someone, he or she will visualize before projecting fear on the person being targeted. The idea that comes just before the physical action of bullying or an unjust act is launched with the frequency of fear. As mentioned earlier, the person committing acts of injustice or bullying uses intimidation as an agent of manipulation to control the person targeted. In my opinion bullying is a form of social injustice. It can be counterproductive from both sides, meaning from the one doing the bullying and the one being bullied.

You may ask why or how does bullying affect the one doing the bullying. The negative energy that is associated with hurting someone for a selfish gain or control can ultimately bring on a strong sense of guilt to the one practicing any form of social injustice. The cycle can be broken when he or she who is acting negatively understands that the pattern of behavior is wrong, along with understanding that it does not make him or her a bad person. Admitting such a fault can be difficult, but it is then that the process of forgiving oneself can begin. The feeling of remorse toward the person targeted is important. However, if there is no compassion towards oneself, without forgiveness of self, it's hard to imagine having or showing compassion toward someone else in a healthy way. Sometimes we give too much attention to people's behavior rather than getting to the root of the problem. There are cycles in the mind that need to be broken and new cycles generated as we become more creative in starting new productive cycles.

Before winning multiple amateur boxing championships, I was bullied as a child. I can think back on situations when I felt the fear, anxiety, confusion, and uncertainty of what was going to happen after school as I sat in class watching the clock. It totally blocked my focus as far as schoolwork was concerned. My thoughts were bombarded with images of situations that involved me getting hurt or possibly even killed. It was just exhausting. All I could see were mental images of what could or would happen. Once again, these were only thoughts.

Even before starting this book I was somewhat bullied with subtle gestures from people when I mentioned the idea of writing on the topic of fear. I was told that it was simply better to write my first book about love, poetry, sports, or entertainment. However, when I watched the news and heard rumors of people who ended their own lives, or of incarcerated individuals who suffered from the pain of social injustice, I said there must be an answer to combat this type of behavior. This book is from the perspective of a person who not only was a victim of social injustice but who also may still be tested to repel even the idea of becoming a victim of this dilemma. Many people are surprised to hear this about my childhood considering I have been involved in combat sports since the age of seven. I started off taking tae kwon do, then moved to jujitsu with Sensei Howard (a former UFC fighter), as I mentioned earlier, then samurai sword fighting, then wrestling, and ultimately boxing. I remember one incident when I and a long line of other students were waiting in line in elementary school to see the nurse. I was consistently being bullied even though I had a background in multiple disciplines. This confirms to me that it is not a physical thing but has more to do with mental projection and perception. At the time I did not see myself as worthy of respect.

His name was Darryl. He was the biggest kid in the class. Bulky and strong. I saw what he did to another kid in the class who was bigger than me yet smaller than Darryl. How he ragdolled him while pounding him in the head at the same time. He seemed to enjoy doing it by the smirk on his face, talking to the poor kid while giving him the brutal beating. People just stood around and watched. I wanted to help, but did not know what to do. This played in my memory as Darryl, the kid who looked like a giant, stood before me. He started off by shoving me and telling me, "I am going to beat you down." He called me so many names that I lost count. At the time, everything that I was going through in life, including domestically, made me feel a sense of hopelessness. I had a moment when I did not care about anything. My focus on the pains of life overtook my rational. Fear of his threats left. I saw red. I somewhat blacked out and found myself swinging and connecting with strikes to his head and body, kicks and punches to the head. I remember people cheering and some laughing as his head snapped back. Darryl stumbled and fell, looking up to me. He began to yell so loud that his voice indicated that he was going to get up and kill me. Suddenly all I could think about was how he ragdolled that other kid. And even though I dominated him physically in a brief moment of combat, fear overtook me, and I ran behind the tables that were set up in the room. When he finally got to his feet, I was smiling, but I was dodging him behind the tables as he shoved them across the room.

I am not promoting violence or saying this was the best way that I could have dealt with the situation. There are alternatives to combat every form of social injustice. It is my belief that the greatest way to overcome social injustice or getting out of the mindset of bullying others, is to find our visions, purposes, and desires to dream. This propels healthy empowerment. This gives motion toward excellence in our thought lives. You are made to be a visionary.

Going back to the story of the little scrap, isn't this just like life? We have conquered some things in life that reveal our potentials to succeed. Yet moments of fear set in and cause us to run away from making our dreams become realities. We run behind everything else, dodging our pursuits along the journey that leads to success. I have been guilty of this, subconsciously creating elements of distractions to dip and hide behind. If you and I have whipped fear once, you can do it again and again. The fact that you are reading this book is an indication that you have a desire to transition to new realms—new places—as you overcome fear. You are attracting something great for your life. Something that will help others. There is greatness already inside you. Elements of fear may have been projected intentionally or unintentionally by those around you. Fear does not discriminate; it can operate through anyone. Even those we look up to may become instruments of fear. Keep in mind when you recognize or identify fear through someone's words or frequency of thoughts, either subtle or blatant, to counteract it by literally saying aloud the opposite. They may say, "You cannot." Then you say, "No, I don't accept that. I can and I will." They may say, "No one has ever done that before." "You say, well, I will be the first person to do it."

Just like going to the gym, lifting weights, running, or building strength, thinking fearlessly needs to be exercised. When you set your mind to do something, there is always a chance of dropping the ball. Pick it up, and give it another try. Remember that we are not failures because we fail. We are only failures if we accept failure as final. Look at you! You don't give up or give in. Your vision and purpose are being renewed. You are going to succeed. I believe in you! You better not stop believing in yourself! Edison said, "Many of life's failures are a result of people who did not realize how close they were to experiencing success when they gave up." Today you get to dream again. Today you get to visualize the desires of your heart without the fear of failure stopping you from making decisions toward the fulfillment of your desire. Whatever you can do today, do not wait until tomorrow. Think fearlessly.

CPSIA information can be obtained
at www.ICGtesting.com
Printed in the USA
BVHW080807200223
R14666500003BA/R146665PG658141BVX00003BA/1